Sir Alex Ferguson:

Inside The Life Of The

Most Successful

Manager of All Time

By

Bobby Michaelson

Sir Alex Ferguson

Sir Alex Ferguson

Table Of Contents

Sir Alex Ferguson

Preface

Sir Alexander Chapman Ferguson CBE, a Scottish former player and manager of football, was born on December 31, 1941. He is best known for leading Manchester United from 1986 to 2013. He is recognized as one of football's all-time great managers and has the most trophies of any manager in the sport's history. With the "Class of '92," who helped make Manchester United one of the richest and most successful clubs in the world in the 1990s, Ferguson is frequently credited with favoring youth throughout his time at the club.

Sir Alex Ferguson

Ferguson was a forward who played for several Scottish teams, such as Dunfermline Athletic and Rangers. He led the Scottish league in goals scored while a player for Dunfermline in the 1965–1966 season. He served as a coach toward the conclusion of his playing career before beginning his managerial career with East Stirlingshire and St Mirren. After that, Ferguson had a very prosperous time managing Aberdeen, taking home three Scottish league titles, four Scottish Cups, and the UEFA Cup Winners' Cup in 1983. After Jock Stein's passing, he took over as Scotland's interim manager and led the team to the 1986 World Cup.

Sir Alex Ferguson

In November 1986, Ferguson was chosen to lead Manchester United. He won 38 trophies over his 26 years with Manchester United, including two UEFA Champions League wins, five FA Cups, and 13 Premier League championships. For his contributions to the game, he received a knighthood in the 1999 Queen's Birthday Honors list.

Ferguson has led Manchester United for the longest time, surpassing Sir Matt Busby's record on December 19, 2010. After his final season, he won the Premier League, and he announced his retirement from management at the end of the 2012–13 campaign.

Sir Alex Ferguson

<u>Early Years</u>

The son of Elizabeth (née Hardie) and
Alexander Beaton Ferguson, was born on
December 31, 1941, at his grandmother's
residence on Shieldhall Road in Glasgow's
Govan neighborhood. His father worked as a
plater's assistant for a shipyard. He lived with
his parents and his younger brother Martin,
who also became a footballer, in a tenement at
667 Govan Road, which has since been
destroyed.

He went to Govan High School after attending
Broomloan Road Primary School.

Sir Alex Ferguson

He started playing football with the Harmony Row Boys Club in Govan, Scotland before moving on to Drumchapel Amateurs, a young organization with a solid track record of turning out senior football players. Also, he served as a union shop steward while serving an apprenticeship as a toolmaker at a plant in Hillington.

Playing Profession

Club

Ferguson began his playing career as a novice with Queen's Park, where he made his striker debut at the age of 16.

He called his debut a "nightmare," however he did score Queen's Park's goal in a 2-1 loss to Stranraer. On Boxing Day 1959, when Queen of the South defeated Queen's Park 7-1, Ivor Broadis, a former England international, was responsible for four of the team's goals. The only goal scorer for Queen's Park was Ferguson.

Sir Alex Ferguson

He played for Queen's Park for 31 games and scored 20 goals, but he was unable to hold down a regular position in the team, thus he went to Saint Johnstone in 1960. Ferguson paired employment in a shipyard in Govan with training at night in Perth while under a part-time contract with St. Johnstone. Although consistently scoring goals for Saint Johnstone, he was unable to hold down a spot in their starting lineup. He frequently asked for transfers, and he even thought about moving to Canada. Ferguson was chosen by the manager for a match against Rangers since Saint Johnstone had been unable to add another forward. Ferguson scored a hat-trick in the unexpected 3-2 victory at Ibrox.

The following summer (1964), Ferguson was signed by Dunfermline, and he started playing football professionally full-time. Dunfermline was a serious contender for the Scottish league title the next season (1964–65), and they advanced to the Scottish Cup Final. However, Ferguson was benched for the final due to his subpar performance in a league match against St Johnstone. Celtic won the championship game 3-2, and Dunfermline fell short of winning the League by one point. Ferguson scored 45 goals in 51 appearances for

Dunfermline in the 1965–1966 season. With 31 goals, he shared the league lead in scoring with Joe McBride of Celtic in Scotland.

Ferguson then made a record-breaking transfer between two Scottish clubs by paying £65,000 to join Rangers.

During his two seasons with the team, he excelled in Europe, scoring six goals in nine appearances in the Inter-Cities Fairs Cup, including two goals against 1. FC Köln in the 1967–68 competition and a crucial goal against Athletic Bilbao in the 1968–69 competition that propelled Rangers into the semi-finals.

However, on both occasions, the English

opposition eliminated Rangers. He was held accountable for a goal that Celtic captain Billy McNeill's squad allowed in the 1969 Scottish Cup Final, and as a result, he was forced to play for the club's junior team rather than the main team. Ferguson reportedly threw away his losers' medal because he was so angry over the event, according to his brother.

There have been allegations that he was treated unfairly at Rangers because of his marriage to Cathy Holding, a Catholic.
Ferguson stated that he "assumed" that his omission from the first team following the 1969 cup final was due to her faith in a 2021

documentary film about his life and career, Sir Alex Ferguson: Never Give In.

Rangers were aware of his wife's religion when he joined the club, according to his memoirs. In March 2021, he added that a Rangers director had inquired as to whether the Fergusons had wed in a (Catholic) chapel when he was signed, and that the director had said, "Well, that's okay," when informed that they had wed in a registry office.

Ferguson unwillingly departed Rangers since he had hoped to succeed there having grown up nearby. He avoided reunions with the Rangers' ex-players because he disliked how when he departed, the media would refer to him as an

"ex-Rangers player."

Ferguson was desired by Nottingham Forest

the following October, but his wife was

opposed to relocating to England at the

moment, so he went to Falkirk. Ferguson spent

four years with Brockville, where he made more

league appearances than he had anywhere else.

He was given a promotion to player-coach in

appreciation of his expertise, but when John

Prentice took over as manager, he did away

with Ferguson's coaching duties. This soured

Ferguson's experience at Falkirk, so he

requested a transfer and moved to Ayr United,

where he concluded his playing career in 1974.

International

The only time Ferguson was associated with

the Scotland national team was during a 1967

international tour. Since the Scottish Football

Association did not recognize any of the tour

games as full internationals for many years,

Ferguson was regarded as having never

represented Scotland.

He was listed as one of the top Scottish players

who had never participated in a complete

international in a June 2020 BBC Sports piece. Ferguson received an international cap after it was declared by the SFA in October 2021 that certain of the tour games would be reclassified as full internationals.

Managerial Career

East Stirlingshire

At the relatively young age of 32, Ferguson was named manager of East Stirlingshire in June 1974. The club at the time had no goalkeepers, thus it was a part-time position paying £40 a week. Bobby McCulley, a club forward, subsequently remarked that he had "never been terrified of anyone before but Ferguson was a terrible bastard from the start" due to his reputation as a strict disciplinarian.

St. Mirren

Ferguson was given the job of managing Saint Mirren in October 1974. Ferguson considered joining East Stirlingshire even though St Mirren was a bigger team and placed lower in the league, but after consulting Jock Stein, he decided to join St Mirren.

During his tenure as St Mirren's manager, which spanned 1974 to 1978, Ferguson oversaw a remarkable turnaround for the club, taking them from a team playing in the bottom half of the old Second Division in front of crowds of just over 1,000 to First Division champions in

1977. Ferguson did this by spotting talents like
Billy Stark, Tony Fitzpatrick, Lex Richardson,
Frank McGarvey, Bobby Reid, and Peter Weir
and directing them to play excellent attacking
football.

The league-winning team's captain,
Fitzpatrick, was 20 years old, while the team's
average age was 19.

The distinction of being the only team to ever
fire Ferguson belongs to St Mirren. At an
employment tribunal, he accused the club of
wrongful dismissal but lost and was denied
permission to appeal. The official explanation,
according to a Sunday Herald report on May 30,

1999, is that Ferguson was fired for several contract violations, including making unauthorized payments to players. He was also charged with pressuring his office assistant because he wanted players to be able to claim some expenses as tax-deductible expenses. He took his keys, went six weeks without speaking to him, and only used a 17-year-old helper. Ferguson was "especially petulant" and "immature," the tribunal found. Ferguson had "no managerial aptitude," according to Saint Mirren chairman Willie Todd, during the tribunal.

The Guardian released an interview with Todd, who had fired Ferguson many years earlier, in 2008. Todd was then 87 years old. According to Todd, Ferguson's agreement to join Aberdeen was a violation of the contract, which served as the primary justification for his dismissal. Jim Rodger of the Daily Mirror said that Ferguson had requested at least one teammate to accompany him to Aberdeen. He announced his departure to the St. Mirren personnel. Todd apologized for what had transpired, but he accused Aberdeen of failing to contact his club to negotiate compensation.

Ferguson declined the Aberdeen manager position in 1977. Billy McNeill was given the post, but after just a year, he returned to Celtic, making room for Ferguson once more.

Aberdeen

The Late 1970s

In June 1978, Ferguson was appointed manager of Aberdeen, taking over for Billy McNeill, who had only led the team for a single season before being allowed to lead Celtic.

Although a major club in Scotland, Aberdeen had only won the league once, in 1955, under

Dave Halliday. Despite finishing second in the league the previous season, the club had been playing well lately and hadn't dropped a league game since the previous December.

Ferguson had been a manager for four years by this point, but he was still relatively young compared to some of the players and struggled to get the respect of some of the more experienced ones, such as Joe Harper.

Aberdeen reached the Scottish Cup semi final and Scottish League Cup final, however, they lost both games and finished fourth in the league, therefore the season did not go particularly well.

Aberdeen was defeated by Dundee United in the 1979–80 Scottish League Cup Final following a replay. Ferguson admitted the loss and said he should have changed the lineup for the replay.

Silverware and the 1980s

Aberdeen had a rough start to the 1979–80 campaign, but things turned around for them in the new year, and they went on to win the Scottish league that year with a 5-0 victory on the last day. For the first time in 15 years, neither Rangers nor Celtic had won the league. Ferguson subsequently remarked:

**"I finally felt that I had the respect of my
players." "That accomplishment served as our
bond. The players eventually started to
believe in me ".**

However, he maintained his tough disciplinary
policies, earning the moniker "Furious Fergie"
from his players. After a subpar first half, he
kicked a tea urn at the players during halftime
and fined one of his players, John Hewitt, for
passing him on a public road.

He was unhappy with the atmosphere at
Aberdeen games and purposefully instilled a
"siege mentality" in the players by claiming

that the Scottish media was biased in favor of the Glasgow clubs.

In 1982, the team won the Scottish Cup, extending their winning streak. The manager's position at Wolverhampton Wanderers was offered to Ferguson, but he declined because he believed Wolves were in trouble and his "ambitions at Aberdeen were not even half realized."

Success in Europe and the Scottish National Team

The following year, 1982–1983, Ferguson guided Aberdeen to even greater glory. They successfully eliminated Bayern Munich, who had defeated Tottenham Hotspur 4-1 in the previous round, after they had qualified for the European Cup Winners' Cup by winning the Scottish Cup the season prior.

According to Willie Miller, this assured them to think they might win the competition, which they achieved by defeating Real Madrid 2-1 in the championship game on May 11, 1983. Ferguson now felt that "he'd done something significant with his life" as Aberdeen became just the third Scottish team to take home a trophy from Europe. When Hamburger SV, the defending European Cup champions, were defeated 2-0 over two legs in the European Super Cup in December 1983, this was followed by triumph. Ferguson was not pleased with his team's performance in that game and angered the players by calling it a "disgraceful performance" in a televised interview after the game, a claim he later withdrew.

Aberdeen had also performed well in the league that season and had won the Scottish Cup with a 1-0 victory over Rangers.

Aberdeen's performance improved after a mediocre start to the 1983–84 campaign, and the squad went on to win the Scottish league and keep the Scottish Cup. In the 1985 New Year's Honours, Ferguson was named an Officer of the Order of the British Empire (OBE) and received managerial offers from Rangers and Arsenal.

Aberdeen won the league again in the 1984–1985 season. Aberdeen won both domestic cups in the 1985-86 season but came in fourth place overall. Ferguson had joined the club's board of directors at the beginning of 1986, but in April he informed chairman Dick Donald that he intended to resign that summer.

Ferguson was a member of the Scottish national team's coaching staff during the 1986

World Cup qualifying process, but manager
Jock Stein passed away on September 10, 1985,
after the match that qualified Scotland from
their group for a play-off against Australia.
Ferguson quickly consented to lead the Scottish
national team against Australia and later at the
World Cup. He appointed Archie Knox to be
his co-manager in Aberdeen so he could fulfill
his international obligations. However,
Ferguson resigned as head coach of the
national team on June 15, 1986, after Scotland
was unable to advance past the World Cup
group round.

Sir Alex Ferguson

Ferguson was allowed to succeed Peter Shreeves as manager around this time by Tottenham Hotspur, but he turned it down. David Pleat of Luton Town was given the position in Ferguson's place. Ferguson was also given the chance to succeed Don Howe as manager of Arsenal, but he turned it down. George Graham, a fellow Scot, was appointed in Ferguson's place. There had been rumors that he would succeed Ron Atkinson at Manchester United, who had fallen to fourth place in the English premier division following a ten-match winning streak.

Ferguson had previously been mentioned in connection with a move to England. When Wolverhampton Wanderers were on the verge of being relegated from the First Division in February 1982, they approached him about taking over as manager in place of John Barnwell. He declined this offer, possibly due to concerns over the club's financial health as they were at the time more than £2 million in debt and almost about to go out of business. When Joe Fagan announced his resignation after the 1984–85 season, it was said that Ferguson was a candidate for the position of Liverpool manager. Nevertheless, Kenny Dalglish, a striker for Liverpool, accepted the position very swiftly.

Ferguson didn't leave Aberdeen during the summer, but after Atkinson was fired in November 1986, he did eventually sign with Manchester United.

Appointment of Manchester United and Winning the Inaugural FA Cup

On November 6, 1986, Ferguson was named manager of Old Trafford.

He was "depressed" by the players' lack of fitness and initially worried that many of them—including Bryan Robson, Paul McGrath, and Norman Whiteside—were drinking too much. However, he was able to improve the players' composure, and United—which had been 21st (second from last) when he took over—climbed the standings to finish the season in 11th place.

His debut game in charge ended in a 2-0 loss at Oxford United on November 8. Seven days later, he managed to draw 0-0 at newly promoted Norwich City before recording his first victory, a 1-0 triumph against Queens Park Rangers at home on November 22. Outcomes improved during the season, and by the time they won at championship rivals and rivals Liverpool on Boxing Day, which would be their sole away victory of the league campaign, it was obvious that United was on the road to recovery.

After a 4-1 victory over Newcastle United to start the season, United gradually came together in the second part of the year, losing only occasionally along the way, and placed 11th in the standings. Three weeks following Ferguson's appointment, his mother Elizabeth passed away at the age of 64 from lung cancer. In 1986, Ferguson appointed Archie Knox, his assistant at Aberdeen, to a similar position at Manchester United.

Ferguson made several significant acquisitions during the 1987–88 campaign, including Steve Bruce, Viv Anderson, and Brian McClair. The new players helped United finish in second place, nine points behind Liverpool, thanks to their contributions. Nonetheless, Liverpool's point advantage had been double digits for the majority of the season, and even though United had only lost five league games all year and had drawn twelve, there was still a long way to go before they could compete with their northwestern rivals.

United competed in two friendly contests in Bermuda during the season against the Somerset Cricket Club and the Bermuda national team.

Ferguson and his assistant Archie Knox both entered the field for the game against Somerset, with Knox even recording a goal. Ferguson played in just one game for Manchester United's starting lineup.

When Jim Leighton and Mark Hughes joined
the team from Aberdeen two years after they
left for Barcelona, expectations for United were
high. However, the 1988–89 campaign was a
disappointment for them as they finished 11th
in the league and lost 1-0 at home to
Nottingham Forest in the FA Cup sixth round.
They had a sluggish start to the season, going
on a nine-match winless streak (with one loss
and eight draws) between October and
November, but a run of generally positive
performances propelled them to third place and
the fringes of the title race by mid-February.
However, they dropped to mid-table in the

remaining three months of the season after another string of poor performances.

Ferguson significantly strengthened his team for the 1989–1990 campaign by spending a lot of money on defender Gary Pallister, winger Danny Wallace, and midfielders Neil Webb, Mike Phelan, and Paul Ince. With a 4-1 victory over the defending champions Arsenal on the first day of the season, United had a strong start, but their league performance gradually declined. In September, United lost at the hands of ferocious rivals Manchester City by a score of 5-1. Following this and a stretch of six losses and two draws in eight games to start the season, a banner at Old Trafford reading "Three years of excuses and it's still trash... ta-ra Fergie" was put up, and many media members and fans called for Ferguson to be fired.

As United finished the decade just outside the relegation zone in December 1989, Ferguson later referred to it as "the saddest period he had ever suffered in the game."

Manchester United was assigned to Nottingham Forest in the third round of the FA Cup after going seven games without a victory. It was anticipated that United would lose the game and Ferguson would be fired as a result because Forest was performing well that season and was on the verge of winning the League Cup for the second consecutive season. However, United defeated Forest 1-0 thanks to a goal from Mark Robins and went on to win the match and advance to the final. Although it has since been claimed that Ferguson's job was never in danger, this cup victory is frequently recognized as the game that preserved his Old Trafford career. After a 3-3 tie in the first game, United went on to win the FA Cup, defeating Crystal Palace 1-0 in the championship replay to give Ferguson his first major trophy as Manchester United manager. Goalkeeper Jim Leighton was cited as the cause of United's defensive shortcomings in the opening game. Ferguson substituted Les Sealey for Leighton in the rematch.

Ferguson's Second-place Finishes and United's firsts in Europe

Even though Newcastle United's league performance much improved in 1990–91, they remained erratic and placed sixth. There were some standout performances that season, such as a 6-2 thrashing of Arsenal at Highbury, but defeats at home to Everton in early March (the match where 17-year-old talented prospect

Ryan Giggs made his senior debut) and early 2-1 losses at newly promoted Sunderland and Liverpool in September and a 4-0 thrashing of Liverpool at Anfield showed that United still had a ways to go.

Even after winning the FA Cup the season before, some people continued to have reservations about Ferguson's potential to do what every other manager since Matt Busby had failed to do: win the league championship. They came in second place in the League Cup after falling to Sheffield Wednesday 1-0. Nonetheless, they defeated the Spanish champions Barcelona 2-1 to win the European

Cup Winners' Cup. That would be the only Cup Winners' Cup victory for United. After the game, Ferguson promised that United would win the league the next season, and after over five years in the position, he finally appeared to have persuaded the last of his doubters.

Ferguson promoted youth team coach Brian Kidd to the position of assistant manager in place of Archie Knox, who left Ferguson's club to join the Rangers as Walter Smith's assistant during the 1991 close season. To strengthen his team, he also made two significant acquisitions: defender Paul Parker and goalkeeper Peter Schmeichel. There was much anticipation for the development of young Ryan Giggs, who had appeared twice and scored once during the 1990–91 season, as well as the earlier rise of Lee Sharpe, another impressive young winger, who had made Ferguson feel like he could resist entering the transfer market and acquiring a new player to replace the underwhelming Danny Wallace on the left wing. In addition, he had moved the veteran midfielders Mike Phelan and Bryan Robson to the right wing, where he had replaced them with the Soviet midfielder Andrei Kanchelskis.

Ferguson's expectations for the 1991–1992 season were not met, many in the media thought that his faults had contributed to the suffering.

Despite dominating the league for the majority of the season, Leeds United won the league championship, and United won the League Cup and European Super Cup for the first time.

A United squad that had played so brilliantly in the first half of the season had been undone by a lack of goals and being held to draws by clubs they had been predicted to beat in the second half of the season. Ferguson believed that United's league title had been lost due to his failure to convince Mick Harford to leave Luton Town and that his club required "an extra dimension" if they were to win the league the following year.

Ferguson began looking for a new striker in the 1992 offseason. In his initial effort, he competed against Blackburn Rovers for the services of Southampton's Alan Shearer. Also, he made at least one attempt to acquire Sheffield Wednesday striker David Hirst, but manager Trevor Francis turned down all bids, therefore the player remained where he was. Dion Dublin, a 23-year-old striker for Cambridge United, was the only significant acquisition he made that summer, and he spent £1 million for him.

After a sluggish start to the 1992–93 campaign,
when United was ranked 10th at the start of
November, it appeared as though they would
lose the league championship again. However,
things started looking up for Manchester
United and Ferguson's job as manager after the
club paid £1.2 million to acquire French striker
Eric Cantona from Leeds. Cantona and Mark
Hughes established a reliable alliance. When
United hosted Sheffield Wednesday on April
10, 1993, they were second in the league. Steve
Bruce's equalizer came with four minutes left in
United's loss. Bruce scored the game-winning
goal in the 97th minute after 7 minutes of

injury time, which was later dubbed "Fergie Time" about extra time allegedly granted to Ferguson's teams to score. Ferguson celebrated the goal by running from his dugout to the touchline while assistant Brian Kidd ran onto the field. It was viewed as a resounding victory that propelled United to the top of the league, where they remained.

The victory made United first Premier League champions and put an end to their 26-year league title drought. United won the championship by ten points over Aston Villa, who ended in second place after United's 1-0 victory at Oldham Athletic on May 2, 1993.

Afterward, the League Managers' Association chose Ferguson as its Manager of the Year.

1993–1995: A Win and a Loss Twice

More achievement came in the 1993–1994 campaign. To replace Bryan Robson, a midfielder who was nearing the end of his career, Ferguson signed 22-year-old Roy Keane from Nottingham Forest for a British record sum of £3.75 million. United essentially held the top spot in the Premier League standings for the 1993–94 season.

Ferguson received the honor for August 1993, making him the inaugural recipient of the Premier League Manager of the Month award, which was instituted at the beginning of the 1993–94 season. Despite receiving two red cards in the space of five days in March 1994, Cantona finished the season as the top scorer with 25 goals across all competitions. Aston Villa, led by Ferguson's predecessor Ron Atkinson, defeated United 3-1 in the League Cup final. Ferguson won his second League and Cup Double with Manchester United in the FA Cup final against Chelsea, following his Scottish Premier Division and Scottish Cup victories with Aberdeen in 1984-85.

Nevertheless, the League Cup loss prevented him from matching the treble he had won with Aberdeen in 1983.

Ferguson only acquired David May from Blackburn for £1.2 million during the offseason. There were newspaper reports that Chris Sutton, a highly regarded 21-year-old striker from Norwich City, was also going to be signed by Ferguson, but he ended up signing with Blackburn.

Ferguson had a more difficult season in 1994–1995. When Cantona attacked a Crystal Palace fan during a match at Selhurst Park, it appeared as though he would quit English football.

Cantona missed the final four months of the season due to an eight-month suspension. For the offense, he was also given a 14-day prison sentence, but that sentence was overturned on appeal and replaced with a 120-hour community service requirement. In return for Andy Cole, a prolific striker for Newcastle United, United paid a British record cost of £7 million, sending teenage winger Keith Gillespie to the region. Young players Gary Neville, Nicky Butt, and Paul Scholes had their breakthroughs during the season and were superb fill-in players for United during the extended absences of some of their more seasoned stars. As Manchester United drew 1-1

with West Ham United on the penultimate day
of the season, when a win would have secured
them a third straight league title, the crown
slipped from their grasp. Everton defeated
United 1-0 in the FA Cup final, which United
also dropped.

1995–98

When three of United's top players were
allowed to leave in the summer of 1995 and no
replacements were acquired, Ferguson received
harsh criticism. First, longtime striker Mark
Hughes was traded to Chelsea for £1.5 million,

then Paul Ince left for Internazionale of Italy, then Andrei Kanchelskis was traded to Everton for £7.5 million. United possessed several young players, in Ferguson's opinion, who were prepared to play for the first team.

Known as "Fergie's Fledglings," the youthful players featured Gary Neville, Phil Neville, David Beckham, Paul Scholes, and Nicky Butt, all of whom would later become significant contributors to the team. And so, amid high-profile signings by teams like Arsenal, Liverpool, and Newcastle, the 1995–96 season got underway without a significant addition.

A young United team fell to Aston Villa 3-1 in the league opener of the 1995-96 campaign. Alan Hansen, a commentator on Match of the Day, criticized their performance and concluded by saying, "You can't win anything with kids."

The return of Cantona, who made his comeback against Liverpool in October 1995, helped United win their following five games. The club had behind league leaders Newcastle for the majority of the season and was ten points behind them by Christmas. This gap was later reduced to seven points after the team defeated Newcastle on December 27, 1995. The difference widened to 12 points, but late in

March, United moved to the top of the standings thanks to a string of victories and Newcastle's loss of ground.

Following Newcastle's victory over Leeds, manager Kevin Keegan reacted strongly to Ferguson's remarks in a televised outburst: "He has to travel to Middlesbrough while we are still competing for the championship. I would adore it if we defeated them." The club defeated Liverpool by a goal to nil in the 1996 FA Cup Final, and a victory over Middlesbrough on the last day won the title for United. This was their second double in three years. A week after the cup final, Ferguson and United agreed on a four-year contract.

Sir Alex Ferguson

Newcastle lost to United 4-0 in the Charity

Shield to kick off the following season.

Newcastle had finished second in the league

the year before. After the 1996–1997 season,

they went on to win their fourth league

championship in five years, which was made

simpler by the fact that their competitors "were

not up to the job."

The squad improved under Ferguson and, for

the first time in 28 years, advanced to the

semifinal round of the Champions League.

After losing to German team Borussia

Dortmund, United did not make any further

progress.

The two significant Norwegian additions to the team were Ole Gunnar Solskjaer and Ronny Johnsen, with the former finishing the season as the team's leading scorer. Cantona notified Ferguson of his decision to stop playing football in May 1997. Ferguson could see why the player "felt used by United's merchandising department" and questioned the club's ambition. Tottenham Hotspur's Teddy Sheringham was acquired as Cantona's replacement, and Blackburn's Henning Berg was the other important acquisition that summer. Keane was named United's new captain during the offseason. After the team's 1997 FA Charity Shield victory, Ferguson called him "the best all-around player in the game" and said Keane had "all the proper components" to flourish after Cantona.

The team's first league defeat in seven months came against Leeds United in September 1997. Keane sustained ligament damage during the game and was forced to miss the remainder of the campaign.

In his absence, goalkeeper Peter Schmeichel was named captain. By November, United had a four-point advantage over the rest of the league, sparking speculation about whether any team could catch them. Ferguson conceded a one-horse race was "not good for the game" after Arsenal defeated United in the same month and said his opponents "...deserved to win on their second-half performance." Despite Arsenal having games in hand, United was able to increase their advantage by 11 points throughout the winter due to the league contenders' mistakes by Liverpool, Chelsea, and Blackburn. This was sufficient for Manchester bookmaker Fred Done to honor wagers made by supporters of the champions keeping their title.

On May 3, 1998, Arsenal defeated Everton to win the title with a perfect score. Ferguson complimented his rival Arsène Wenger, who later completed the double in his first full season with the team:

"For my young players to lose this game, I believe, is beneficial. I applaud what Arsenal accomplished from the holiday season till the end of the campaign."

Jaap Stam, a defender for PSV, was immediately acquired by United for a new club record sum of £10.75 million. Ferguson set his sights on Dwight Yorke of Aston Villa to improve the team's offensive options. Initially, attempts to sign Yorke were unsuccessful, but Ferguson eventually persuaded Edwards to accept

United's higher offer of £10 million. A week into the league season, a £12.6 million agreement was made, and Yorke signed just before the cutoff time for submitting United's team for the Champions League.

1998–99: Triple Success

In the 1998 FA Charity Shield, United lost to Arsenal 3-0 to start the 1998–99 campaign. Ferguson seemed unconcerned about the thumping, even though he found his team's loss to Arsenal in September 1998 to be "a lot less palatable."

Kidd resigned his position as an assistant in December 1998 to take over as manager of Blackburn Rovers. Ferguson gave Les Kershaw and Eric Harrison instructions to identify replacements who were "appropriate in terms of coaching skill and work ethic." Both individuals endorsed Steve McClaren, Jim Smith's Derby County assistant. Ferguson first selected McClaren and appointed him in February 1999. The 8-1 triumph over Nottingham Forest by United was his debut match in the role of assistant.

Because of their commitments to other tournaments, Ferguson believed United's attempt to win back the Premier League started uneventfully. The squad finished second in their "group of death" in the Champions League, behind Bayern Munich and ahead of Barcelona, and he was willing to "pay for the progress" made there. The FA Cup fourth-round victory over Liverpool by United was an omen for the rest of the campaign. After falling behind 1-0 after three minutes, the squad tied the score in the 86th, and in extra time, Solskjaer scored the game-winning goal. Ferguson later observed, "A manifestation of the morale that was to be every bit as crucial as rich skill in the five months that lay ahead of United," after reflecting on the incident.

In the 1998-99 season, United won three titles under Ferguson.

Arsenal became a respectable United rival in the waning weeks of the league season. In the FA Cup semifinal, which was decided by a replay after the first game ended scoreless, the two clubs were also drawn together. United gave up a penalty late in the game with the score still tied at 1 after Keane was dismissed in the second half. Peter Schmeichel was able to stop Dennis Bergkamp's effort. Giggs sprinted the length of the field and avoided numerous Arsenal players to score the game-winning goal in extra time, contrary to Ferguson's hopes that his team "could at least take it to a penalty shoot-out."

After winning the Premiership title back a week earlier, United went on to defeat Newcastle United in the FA Cup final to clinch the double.

Compared to past seasons, United's development in the Champions League was encouraging. In the quarterfinal round, the team defeated Inter Milan, and in the final four, they met Juventus. After giving up an away goal in the first leg, Giggs' late strike secured the team a 1-1 tie, but Ferguson remained confident in his side's chances to advance to the championship game: "I have a feeling that we will prevail. Because of the way, we torment ourselves in our club, winning there is the only way to feel better."

Striker Filippo Inzaghi scored twice in the Stadio delle Alpi to give Juventus a 3-1 aggregate lead. Just before halftime, Keane headed in a Beckham cross to lessen the deficit, but he was later given a yellow card for a foul on Edgar Davids, excluding him from the championship game. Yorke brought the score even before Cole added a third to seal the victory. Ferguson gave Keane credit for his performance:

I have never witnessed a football field exhibition of selflessness quite like it. He motivated everyone around him by stomping on every blade of grass and competing as though he would rather pass out from exhaustion than lose. Being linked with a player of his caliber seemed honorable to me.

United visited Barcelona, the site of the UEFA Champions League final, a few days after the FA Cup final. Scholes and Keane's suspensions prevented them from playing against Bayern Munich, so Ferguson debated his team lineup. The manager thought Beckham playing in center midfield would prevent the opposition from playing narrow, so Giggs was shifted to the right wing and Blomqvist started on the left. In the first six minutes of the championship, United gave up a free kick from Mario Basler. In the opening minute of extra time, Sheringham, who replaced Blomqvist, scored from a corner to tie the score. Ferguson responded, "Steve, this game isn't over," when McClaren instructed him to organize the players for extra time. Solskjr's game-winning goal came three minutes into the extra time, giving United an unprecedented treble. Ferguson stated when questioned shortly after, "It's just unbelievable. Bloody heck, football. It was won, though, because they resisted giving in." During the award ceremony, he and the acting captain Schmeichel lifted the cup collectively.

Almost 500,000 people gathered in Manchester's streets to welcome the players as they paraded through the city in an open-top bus.

United was allowed to compete in the Intercontinental Cup as the European Champions. The club also participated in Brazil's first Club World Championship. As a result, United, the first FA Cup holders to do so, accepted the FA's proposal to withdraw from the competition to avoid a potential schedule overload. Later, Ferguson expanded on the choice made by the team: "To aid England's World Cup bid, we did it. The political climate was as it was. We had nothing but stick and demeaning comments for not making the FA Cup when, in reality, it wasn't our fault, so I felt sorry."

1999–2002: Retirement Plan, a Hat-trick of Titles

Following Schmeichel's decision to quit United after eight seasons, Ferguson brought in Mark Bosnich from Aston Villa and Italian Massimo

Taibi as Schmeichel's successors. The latter played in four games, the latest of which was a 5-0 loss against Chelsea in October 1999; Ferguson did not pick him again. With just three losses and a league-record 18 points in the lead, United won the 1999–2000 season. The club defeated Palmeiras in Tokyo to win the Intercontinental Cup in December 1999, but one month later they were eliminated from the first Club World Championship in the group stage. Despite Ferguson's declaration that the competition was "great," United was unable to defend its Champions League title after falling to eventual champion Real Madrid in the quarterfinals. To improve his team, Ferguson spent £7.8 million to acquire Fabien Barthez from Monaco. Ruud van Nistelrooy, "a striker of the finest level," was another player he kept an eye on. When they met in Manchester to discuss paperwork, he learned about Van Nistelrooy's problematic right knee. Ferguson was unfazed by this because he knew from previous experience that a comparable ache did not end his playing career. After failing his physical, Van Nistelrooy was comforted by Ferguson, who said, "We might yet find a way out of the nightmare." In April 2001, the transaction was revived for a British transfer record transfer fee of £19 million.

Sir Alex Ferguson

United won the league championship for a
third consecutive season in 2000–01, making
them just the fourth team in history to do so.
The triumph was overshadowed by rumors of a
disagreement between Ferguson and the club's
board of directors. After his contract expired
the following year, he made the following
statement to the club's television station,
MUTV:

**"The choice has already been made. I'm
getting out of here. I was hoping something
would be resolved, therefore I'm unhappy
with what's transpired. Simply put, it hasn't
happened the way I anticipated it would."**

Both sides eventually came to an agreement that Ferguson was happy with:

"I'm glad we were able to resolve this. When you spend as much time at the club as I have, it becomes ingrained in your blood."

Ferguson's choice to retire was influenced by several factors, including his age. Reaching 60 created a "psychological barrier" and altered his perception of his fitness and health. When McClaren moved to manage Middlesbrough in May 2001, Jimmy Ryan was designated Ferguson's assistant for the balance of the season.

With the reported £28.1 million acquisition of Juan Sebastián Verón from Lazio, United once more shattered their transfer record. Stam was traded to Lazio in August 2001 for £16 million. The player supposedly transferred as a result of assertions made by Stam in his memoirs Head to Head, according to which Ferguson was improperly contacted about a move to Manchester United before PSV was informed. Ferguson claimed that he had to sell the player to reduce the team's "huge pay expenditure."

He brought in Laurent Blanc, a long-desired target, to replace the defense.

Eight years later, in an interview with Alastair Campbell, Ferguson revealed that his biggest error at the club was "releasing Jaap Stam. With no doubt ".

With a home loss to West Ham in December 2001, the team had a terrible first half of the season and remained in ninth place.

Ferguson put his retirement plans on hold the evening before Christmas. His family persuaded him to continue leading United, and the following day Ferguson informed Watkins of his about-face.

United's performance improved after Ferguson made his choice to stay public in February 2002. Despite winning 13 of its 15 games, the team only managed to finish third in the league behind Liverpool and Arsenal. In Europe, United was unsuccessful, falling to Bayer Leverkusen in the semifinals of the Champions League by away goals. They finished the season without any trophies due to early exits from the League Cup and FA Cup. Ferguson said that his choice to retire hurt the players and his capacity to enforce punishment.

2002–2006: Reconstruction and Change

Ferguson hired Carlos Queiroz as his new assistant in June 2002.

Andy Roxburgh suggested at a time when United was looking for players from the southern hemisphere and in need of a multilingual coach. Ferguson gave Queiroz the position "straight away" following their first encounter because he was so impressed. Rio Ferdinand was acquired by United for £29.3 million in July 2002 from Leeds United. The team once again smashed the record for British transfers, although Ferguson was unconcerned about this: "We have the right to strive and develop ourselves, and there's nothing wrong with that."

In August 2003, United acquired Cristiano Ronaldo.

United had a relatively dismal start to the 2002–03 season; it was the team's worst start to a league campaign in 13 years.

Ferguson "will recognize this challenging start to the season for what it is: the greatest challenge of his career," Hansen said in a column for The Daily Telegraph. Ferguson's remark was as bombastic as usual:

I'm not compensated to be anxious. There have been many halting beginnings. The situation right now is not my biggest challenge. My biggest obstacle was removing Liverpool from their fucking throne. You can print that as well.

During this time, Ferguson "slightly gambled" by sending many players abroad for surgery in the hopes that they would return reenergized. A loss against Manchester City at Maine Road in November 2002 was one of the defeats that compelled United to alter their playing strategy. To accommodate Diego Forlán, the squad "pushed the ball forward more quickly rather than focussing on possession ratios," and the coaching staff initially tested Ruud van Nistelrooy before landing on Paul Scholes. After losing to Liverpool in the 2003 Football League Cup Final, United's league performance improved throughout the season, and in May 2003, they outclassed Arsenal to win the Premier League for the ninth time. Real Madrid defeated the squad in two legs to knock them out of the Champions League quarterfinal; Ferguson called the second game, a 4-3 victory at Old Trafford, "awesome."

In June 2003, Queiroz left United after one season to take over as manager of Real Madrid.

Ferguson did not designate a replacement because he believed his deputy would return — "Three months later, he was wanting to flee Madrid." While Juan Sebastian Verón joined Chelsea, David Beckham also transferred to Real Madrid during the summer. In the meanwhile, United reconstructed their roster, replacing Barthez in goal with Tim Howard and adding Kléberson, Eric Djemba-Djemba, and Cristiano Ronaldo to the lineup. Had Ronaldinho "not answered yes, then no, to our offer," he might have also accepted.

Rio Ferdinand was given an eight-month football playing suspension in December 2003 after he skipped a drug test. Ten years later, Ferguson accused the drug testers in his autobiography "didn't perform their duties. They did not search for Rio ".

United's 2003–04 Premier League title defense was affected by Ferdinand's absence; the club finished third, behind Chelsea and Arsenal's "Invincibles." They were defeated by the eventual champions Porto in Europe. Ferguson believed it was possible "not because of the players' performance but because of the referee," who rejected a true Scholes goal that would have been sufficient to advance. After defeating Millwall 3-0 in the 2004 FA Cup final,

United finished the season as the cup's champion.

Young striker Wayne Rooney, who cost more than £20 million, and Argentine defender Gabriel Heinze joined United at the start of the 2004–05 season, and Cristiano Ronaldo continued his previous season's trend of producing more game-winning performances. Nonetheless, the club's third third-place result in four seasons was due to the lack of a striker after Ruud van Nistelrooy missed most of the season due to injury. They lost to Arsenal on penalties in the FA Cup final in 2004–2005.

2004–05 marked an unusual instance of a trophyless season for United due to Milan's second-round elimination from the Champions League and Chelsea's semifinal elimination from the League Cup (who also won the Premier League title). Ferguson oversaw United's 2-1 home victory over Lyon during the season, which marked his 1,000th game in charge of the team.

The ownership of the racehorse Rock of Gibraltar was the subject of a high-profile disagreement between Ferguson and major stakeholder John Magnier, which interfered with Ferguson's plans for the 2005–06 season.

Malcolm Glazer was able to take over full ownership of the club after Magnier and his business partner J. P. McManus decided to sell their stakes to Glazer. Ferguson's plans to strengthen the club in the transfer market were derailed by the United fans' violent protests in response to this. Despite this, United sought to fix their midfield and goalkeeping issues. For this, they acquired the services of Korean superstar Park Ji-sung from PSV and Dutch goalkeeper Edwin van der Sar from Fulham.

The season was a time of change. Roy Keane's contract was mutually terminated on November 18, the day he officially left the team. United was unable to advance to the UEFA Champions League knockout round. After signing French fullback Patrice Evra and Serbian defender Nemanja Vidic during the January transfer window, the team placed second in the league, trailing league champion Chelsea. The League Cup victory served as a consolation for the team's lack of other achievements. After being benched in the League Cup final, Ruud van Nistelrooy's position at Old Trafford was in jeopardy, and he left the club at the end of the campaign.

Ferguson faced a lot of backlash before the start of the new season, particularly in the form of a story in The Guardian headed "Shredding his legacy at every turn."

Another Champions League Championship

Roy Keane left the team in 2006, and Michael Carrick was brought in to replace him for a sum that would eventually reach £18 million.

United had a strong start to the season, winning their first four Premier League games for the first time, their best start since 1985. From the tenth game of the 38-game season, they established the early pace in the Premier

League and never lost the top spot. The January 2006 acquisitions, of Patrice Evra and Nemanja Vidic, along with Rio Ferdinand and captain Gary Neville, had a significant impact on United's results. With the addition of Carrick, Paul Scholes was given more room to be creative and the United midfield became more stable. By significantly enhancing the pace and incisiveness of the attack with Wayne Rooney and Cristiano Ronaldo, Park Ji-sung and Ryan Giggs both demonstrated their importance to the first-team group.

On November 6, 2006, Ferguson honored the 20th anniversary of his employment as

Manchester United manager. Both former and current members of Ferguson's team, as well as his old rival Arsène Wenger, paid tribute to him. The celebration was ruined the following day as United lost to Southend United by a score of one goal in the League Cup's fourth round.

On December 1, it was revealed that Manchester United had signed Henrik Larsson, 35, on a loan deal. Ferguson had long admired and tried to buy Larsson in the past. Cristiano Ronaldo scored the club's 2,000th goal under Ferguson on December 23, 2006, in a game against Aston Villa.

Later, Manchester United won their ninth Premier League championship, but Didier Drogba's late goal in the FA Cup final at Wembley Stadium prevented them from completing an unprecedented fourth double. The team advanced to the semifinals of the Champions League, defeating Roma 7-1 at home in the second leg of the quarterfinal, but fell to Milan 3-0 at the San Siro in the second leg of the semifinal after leading 3-2 after the first leg.

Ferguson made significant signings to strengthen United's starting lineup for the 2007–08 campaign. Long-term aim Owen

Hargreaves signed from Bayern Munich, promising Portuguese winger Nani and Brazilian playmaker Anderson soon after, and the final signing of the summer was Carlos Tevez of West Ham and Argentina following a convoluted and drawn-out transfer drama.

After defeating Chelsea in the Community Shield to exact some revenge, United had their worst start to a league campaign under Ferguson, drawing their first two games before losing 1-0 to neighborhood rivals Manchester City. United, on the other hand, bounced back and started a close title chase with Arsenal. After a string of victories, Ferguson declared that this was the best team he has put together at Manchester United thus far in his tenure there.

At Old Trafford, United defeated Arsenal 4-0 in an FA Cup fifth-round game on February 16, 2008, however, on March 8, 2008, eventual champion Portsmouth defeated United 1-0 to advance to the quarterfinals. Ferguson claimed after the game that Keith Hackett, general manager of the Professional Game Match Officials Board, was "not performing his job correctly" after United's penalty claim was denied. Ferguson then faced an improper conduct allegation from The FA, which he chose to fight. Ferguson had already been charged once this year for complaining to the referee when United lost 1-0 at Bolton Wanderers, a charge he chose not to appeal.

On May 11, 2008, exactly 25 years to the day after he had led Aberdeen to victory against Real Madrid in the Cup Winners' Cup, Ferguson guided Manchester United to its tenth Premier League title. The closest competitor Chelsea, which was two points behind the winner coming into the last round of games but had a better goal differential, could only draw 1-1 at home to Bolton. After a 2-0 victory over Wigan Athletic, inspired by former United captain Steve Bruce, United officially won the league.

Ferguson won his second European Cup with Manchester United on May 21, 2008, when they defeated Chelsea 6-5 on penalties in the Luzhniki Stadium in Moscow, ending the first-ever all-English UEFA Champions League Final with a 1-1 draw after extra time. In the end, Edwin van der Sar's blocking of a Nicolas Anelka penalty delivered the trophy to Manchester United for the second time under Ferguson and for the third time overall after Cristiano Ronaldo missed his opportunity, which would have given the trophy to Chelsea if it had been successfully converted.

World champions and Additional League Championships

Ferguson became the first manager in English football history to win the Premier League three times in a row, on two different occasions, despite the team's sluggish start to the 2008–09 campaign. United clinched the league with one game remaining. Manchester United have now won 11 league championships under Ferguson, and their 2008–09 title victory tied Liverpool for the most league championships (18) ever. After becoming the first British team to win the FIFA Club World Cup in December 2008, they also defeated Tottenham in the League Cup final and prevailed on penalties following a scoreless draw.

On May 27, 2009, they faced Barcelona in the Champions League final; they lost 2-0, failing to retain the cup.

Ferguson added another League Cup to his list of accomplishments during the 2009–10 season when United overcame Aston Villa 2-1 in the championship game on February 28, 2010, marking the team's first-ever successful knockout cup defense. His hopes of winning a third European Cup, however, were dashed a few weeks later when United was eliminated from the competition by Bayern Munich on away goals. And on the last day of the season, Chelsea defeated United to win the Premier League by one point, defeating Wigan Athletic 8-0 and making United's 4-0 victory against Stoke City pointless, ending their dreams of a record-breaking 19th league title.

He surpassed Liverpool's record of 18 at the end of the next season by winning his 12th league championship and Manchester United's

19th. On May 28, 2011, Manchester United and Barcelona squared off again in the third Champions League final in four years. This time, Manchester United was defeated 3-1. According to analyst Alan Hansen, Ferguson was "the essential element" in United's success that year, so important that "he would have claimed the title with any of the other top sides had he been in charge of them," according to Alan Hansen. Following the retirements of Edwin van der Sar, Gary Neville, and Paul Scholes in 2011, Sir Alex Ferguson splashed out by acquiring goalkeeper David de Gea from Atlético Madrid for about £19 million, along with defenders Phil Jones from Blackburn and Ashley Young from Aston Villa.

The next year, United defeated City in the 2011 FA Community Shield and defeated them in the third round of the FA Cup, but they still finished the season behind City, who went on to win their first Premier League championship based on goal differential. Ferguson was inspired by this heartbreaking and narrow loss to buy star striker Robin van Persie from another archrival Arsenal on August 17, 2012. Van Persie was the Premier League Golden Boot champion.

Ferguson led United to their 20th league title during the 2012–13 season after beating Aston Villa 3-0 at home on April 22, 2013, with four games remaining. Van Persie scored all three goals in the first half to collect the Golden Boot once again.

His 1,500th and final game in charge saw United and West Bromwich Albion play to a 5-5 tie. As a result, United finished the season 11 points ahead of Manchester City, who finished second. Ferguson presided over United against Southampton on September 2, 2012, to manage his 1,000th league game. With another hat-trick from Van Persie, United prevailed 3-2 in the contest. Two weeks later, he defeated

Galatasaray 1-0 at Old Trafford to win his 100th

match in the Champions League.

<u>Retirement</u>

Ferguson said on May 8, 2013, that he will step down from his position as manager after the football season, but would continue to serve as a director and club ambassador.

The Guardian declared it to be the "end of an era", while Michel Platini, the president of UEFA, called Ferguson "a great visionary." Paul Ince and Bryan Robson, both ex-players for Manchester United, concurred that Ferguson would be "a hard act to follow." Joel Glazer, the co-chairman of Manchester United, remarked, "His tenacity and commitment to the team have been simply exceptional."

Ferguson admitted that it had been extremely difficult for him to keep his retirement plans a secret and that he had chosen to retire back in December 2012. United's stock on the New York Stock Exchange dropped 5% as a result of Ferguson's decision to retire.

On May 9, 2013, Manchester United confirmed that David Moyes, the manager of Everton, would take over as the club's manager on July 1 after signing a six-year contract. Romelu Lukaku, a future United player, scored a hat-trick as Manchester United and West Bromwich Albion drew 5-5 in Ferguson's final game in charge.

In October 2013, Ferguson published My Autobiography, his second autobiography. Ferguson was named the UEFA Coaching Ambassador in January 2014 and described the position as "an honor and a responsibility." Ferguson accepted a "long-term teaching post" at Harvard University in April 2014, where he would provide lectures on a brand-new subject named "The Business of Entertainment, Media, and Sports."

In a series of interviews with Anita Elberse, he claimed his success formula was published in the Harvard Business Review six months prior. In partnership with billionaire entrepreneur, author, and former journalist Michael Moritz,

he released his book, Leading: Lessons from

Life and My Years at Manchester United, in

August 2015.

Controversies

Graham Gordon

Gordon Strachan was a crucial player for Ferguson at Aberdeen, but the two fell out after Strachan secretly accepted a contract with FC Köln in Germany. Ferguson stated that despite Strachan's "cunning nature, I had never anticipated that he could pull such a stroke on me".

In the summer of 1984, Strachan relocated to Manchester United rather than signing with Köln.

Strachan appreciated the decision because, in contrast to Ferguson, he thought Ron Atkinson treated him like an adult. When Ferguson was chosen as the club's manager in November 1986, Strachan was still working there. Ferguson traded Strachan to Leeds United in 1989 because he believed Strachan did not play for United with the same assurance he did in Scotland. As an experienced player, Strachan had great success with Leeds, helping them defeat Ferguson's United to win the English league title in 1991–1992.

As Strachan transitioned into management, their relationship remained chilly. According to

Sir Alex Ferguson

Ferguson's 1999 autobiography, Strachan

"could not be trusted an inch - I would not

want to show my back to him in a hurry."

In his autobiography, My Life in Football,

Strachan described his response to the attack as

being "surprised and disappointed," though he

had a sneaking suspicion that Ferguson had

assisted in the relegation of Strachan's

Coventry City in 2001 by fielding a depleted

Manchester United squad in a game against

Derby County. Before United's Champions

League matches against Strachan's Celtic in

2006, they appeared to have "announced

something of a truce".

Davud Beckham

David Beckham and Ferguson got into a fight in the locker room in February 2003 while playing for Manchester United.

Beckham allegedly suffered a slight injury to his face when Ferguson allegedly booted a football boot, out of fury. Beckham received an apology from Ferguson before being moved to Real Madrid later that year.

Fixing of Champions League Draws

Ferguson asserted that the Champions League draw was rigged in favor of Spanish and Italian teams on April 5, 2003.

Ferguson was accused by UEFA of defaming the sport with his remarks. Ferguson expressed regret for his comments and explained in a letter to UEFA, but the organization nonetheless fined him 10,000 Swiss francs (£4,600).

Gibraltar Rock

Ferguson filed a lawsuit in 2003 over the stud privileges for racehorse Rock of Gibraltar against John Magnier, who was then a significant shareholder at Manchester United. By filing a "Motion to Comply," which demanded that Ferguson provide evidence to support his demand for half of Rock of

Gibraltar's stud fees, Magnier counter-sued Ferguson. Magnier's ownership of a sizable portion of the football team then under Ferguson's management added to the legal complications. Magnier asked for "99 Questions" about Ferguson's transfers of Jaap Stam, Juan Sebastián Verón, Tim Howard, David Bellion, Cristiano Ronaldo, and Kléberson to be answered. The dispute was ultimately resolved outside of court.

BBC

After a program titled Fergie and Son aired on BBC Three on May 27, 2004, Ferguson declined to give interviews to the BBC.

The documentary "portrayed his agent son, Jason, as someone who misused his father's status and position to his objectives on the transfer market," according to an article in The Independent. Jason was never found guilty of any misconduct, as was made plain in the same newspaper piece, which also quoted Alex Ferguson as saying:

"They the BBC produced an absurd story about my son. Everything was made up, including the "brown paper bags" and other carry-on items. It was a terrible insult to my son's honor, and he shouldn't have ever been held accountable for it."

His aides, most recently Mike Phelan, conducted further interviews for BBC programs including Match of the Day.

Ferguson was compelled to halt his BBC boycott following new Premier League regulations slated for the 2010–11 season. Nonetheless, he continued to boycott, and Manchester United announced they would cover the associated fines.

As the BBC wanted to settle the argument, no fines were ever imposed. Ferguson agreed to halt his seven-year boycott after meeting with BBC director general Mark Thompson and BBC

North director Peter Salmon on August 25, 2011.

Referees

Ferguson has been subject to several sanctions for verbally insulting and publicly criticizing match officials when he believed they were at fault.

—**On October 20, 2003**, a touchline penalty of two games and a £10,000 fine were imposed when fourth official Jeff Winter was subjected to verbal abuse and/or insults.

—**14 December 2007** - Two-match touchline suspension and a £5,000 fine for making derogatory remarks about Mark Clattenburg.

—**18 November 2008** - Two-match touchline suspension and a £10,000 fine following an altercation with Mike Dean following a game.

—**12 November 2009** - Four-match touchline suspension (with two games being postponed) and a £20,000 fine for comments made regarding Alan Wiley's fitness.

—**16 March 2011** - Five-match touchline ban (three plus the two suspended for the aforementioned offense) and a £30,000 fine for remarks that questioned Martin Atkinson's performance and fairness.

The "Fergie Time"

Also, it has been asserted that Ferguson's intimidation of officials contributed to the addition of "Fergie Time," or excessively long injury time, in games where Manchester United trailed. The expression dates back to at least 2004, but the idea first appeared on April 10, 1993, when Steve Bruce scored a goal against Sheffield Wednesday in the 97th minute, which was the seventh minute of added injury time by the referee. United went to the top of the league with this victory and remained there until the end of the season.

When games appeared to be taking longer than expected due to injuries, the idea began to circulate in the media (and among opponents). The Times' statistical research raises the possibility that this idea is real, but the article also notes that other footballing factors might account for the association between extra time and United's deficit.

According to Opta Sports' analysis of Premier League games from 2010 to 2012, games that Manchester United was losing to lasted 79 seconds longer on average. Although most of these clubs appear to benefit from a "Fergie Time" impact, particularly at their home

Sir Alex Ferguson

matches, this was a higher number than for
other elite clubs.

Legacy

Ferguson, carrying on Manchester United's heritage under Sir Matt Busby is on exhibit at the National Football Museum.

Ferguson's former players include Tony Fitzpatrick, Alex McLeish, Gordon Strachan, Mark McGhee, Willie Miller, Neale Cooper, Bryan Gunn, Eric Black, Billy Stark, Bryan Robson, Steve Bruce, Mark Hughes, Roy Keane, Paul Ince, Chris Casper, Mark Robins, Jesse Lingard, Gary Neville, Paul Scholes, Ryan Giggs, David Healy, Gabriel Heinze, Paul Scholes, and Ole Gunnar Sol

Three of them went on to coach Manchester United: Carrick (from 2018 to 2021), Solskjr (interim player-manager in 2014), and Giggs (interim manager in 2021).

The Collins English Dictionary and the Oxford English Dictionary now both feature the expression "squeaky-bum time," which Ferguson invented to describe the heated conclusion of league competition.

On November 23, 2012, a bronze statue of Ferguson created by Scottish artist Philip Jackson was unveiled in front of Old Trafford.

Ferguson attended a ceremony on October 14, 2013, to rename a street at Old Trafford from Water's Reach to Sir Alex Ferguson Way. Aberdeen paid sculptor Andy Edwards to create a bronze statue of Ferguson, which was unveiled in July 2021. On February 25, 2022, it was revealed at Pittodrie Stadium in Aberdeen. The next day, Ferguson was given a maquette of the statue.

Sir Alex Ferguson: Never Give In, a documentary about Ferguson's life, debuted in UK theaters on May 27, 2021, and on May 29, it became accessible on Amazon Prime Video in the UK and Ireland. Interviews with Ferguson himself, his family, his doctors, and former players that he oversaw during his career are also included.

<u>Personal Life</u>

Ferguson and his wife Cathy (née Holding) reside in Wilmslow, Cheshire. Three boys were born to their 1966 marriage: Mark (born in 1968), the twins Darren (born in 1972), a former professional football player who most recently served as manager of Peterborough United, and Jason, who owns an event planning business. Sir Alex Ferguson: Never Give Up, a documentary about his father, was directed by Jason in 2021.

Ferguson's name appeared on a list of the largest individual donations to the Labour Party in 1998.

He calls himself a socialist.

A supporter of Manchester United and Labour MP for Manchester Graham Stringer proposed the creation of a life peerage for Ferguson in January 2011. Following Ferguson's announcement of his retirement in May 2013, Stringer and colleague Manchester Labour MP Paul Goggins reiterated this appeal.

Sir Alex Ferguson

From Manchester Metropolitan University, Ferguson was awarded an honorary doctorate in business administration in 2009.

In addition to his ambassadorial duties at Manchester United, numerous public speaking engagements, and charitable commitments in his later years, he has been a longtime supporter of his boyhood team Harmony Row and led a successful effort to raise money for the organization to build new facilities (they are now based at Braehead).

Ferguson favored Scotland staying a part of the United Kingdom in the 2014 Scottish independence referendum.

He criticized Alex Salmond, the First Minister of Scotland, for denying Scots residing in the United Kingdom but outside of Scotland the right to vote.

He also disagreed with the Yes Scotland campaign's self-imposed prohibition on taking contributions of more than £500 from those living outside of Scotland, which they pushed the No campaign to follow as well.

On May 5, 2018, Ferguson needed an urgent procedure following a cerebral hemorrhage. He

recovered from the procedure, and on
September 22, 2018, he went to his first game at
Old Trafford since.

Ferguson started collecting wine in 1991 after
visiting Montpellier, France, and being shown a
collection of bottles from Château d'Yquem
and Château Pétrus.

He offered a portion of his sizable collection up
for auction with Christie's in 2014, with their
director of wine David Elswood praising his
"excellent" taste and estimating it to be worth
up to £3 million. Ferguson sold 229 pieces for
£2.2 million in the first of three auctions.

Sir Alex Ferguson

Honors

Playing at St Johnstone

—Scottish Division Two: Falkirk 1962–1963

—Scottish Division Two: Individual 1969–1970

—Scottish Separation Only one top scorer:

1965–1966

—2006–2007: Dunfermline Athletic Hall of

Fame

—October 2012: Queen's Park Lifetime

Membership Award

Manager

Sir Alex Ferguson

—In 2002, Ferguson was named the first inductee into the English Football Hall of Fame in honor of his managerial contributions to the English game.

—Ferguson was the first person to receive the FA Coaching Diploma, which is given to coaches with at least 10 years of experience as managers or head coaches, in 2003.

—He serves as the Vice-President of the National Football Museum in Manchester and is a member of the League Managers Association's Executive Committee.

Sir Alex Ferguson

—In recognition of Sir Alex Ferguson's 25 years as Manchester United manager, the Old Trafford North Stand has formally renamed the Sir Alex Ferguson Stand on November 5, 2011.

—In addition to being the last manager to win the Scottish league championship with a team other than the Old Firm, Aberdeen did so in the 1984–85 season.

—He is the only manager to win the top league honors, and the "Double," north and south of England–Scotland border (winning the Premier League with Manchester United, and the Scottish Premier Division with Aberdeen).

Sir Alex Ferguson

—With seven awards, Ferguson is the second-most awarded manager in European football leagues, just behind Carlo Ancelotti.

—Ferguson set a record by winning England's first-division crown 13 times.

—He is also the only manager in English league history to twice win three straight league championships.

—Ferguson oversaw the most games in the UEFA Champions League and received 27

Manager of the Month honors in addition to 10 Manager of the Year awards (190).

—Ferguson was listed as one of the top ten coaches since UEFA's founding in 1954 in 2017.

Trophies

St Mirren

—Scottish First Division: 1976–77

Aberdeen

—Scottish Premier Division: 1979–80, 1983–84, 1984–85

—Scottish Cup: 1981–82, 1982–83, 1983–84,

1985–86

Scottish League Cup: 1985–86

—Drybrough Cup: 1980

—European Cup Winners' Cup: 1982–83

—European Super Cup: 1983

Manchester United

—Premier League: 1992–93, 1993–94, 1995–96,

1996–97, 1998–99, 1999–2000, 2000–01, 2002–03,

2006–07, 2007–08, 2008–09, 2010–11, 2012–13.

—FA Cup: 1989–90, 1993–94, 1995–96, 1998–99,

2003–04.

Sir Alex Ferguson

—Football League Cup: 1991–92, 2005–06, 2008–09, 2009–10.

—FA Charity/Community Shield: 1990 (shared), 1993, 1994, 1996, 1997, 2003, 2007, 2008, 2010, 2011.

—UEFA Champions League: 1998–99, 2007–08; runner-up: 2008–09, 2010–11

—European Cup Winners' Cup: 1990–91

—European Super Cup: 1991

—Intercontinental Cup: 1999

—FIFA Club World Cup: 2008.

Sir Alex Ferguson

Individual

—LMA Manager of the Decade: 1990s

&LMA Manager of the Year: 1992–93, 1998–99,

2007–08, 2010–11, 2012–13.

—LMA Special Merit Award: 2009, 2011.

—Premier League Manager of the Season:

1993–94, 1995–96, 1996–97, 1998–99, 1999–2000,

2002–03, 2006–07, 2007–08, 2008–09, 2010–11,

2012–13.

—Premier League Manager of the Month:

August 1993, October 1994, February 1996,

March 1996, February 1997, October 1997,

January 1999, April 1999, August 1999, March
2000, April 2000, February 2001, April 2003,
December 2003, February 2005, March 2006,
August 2006, October 2006, February 2007,
January 2008, March 2008, January 2009, April
2009, September 2009, January 2011, August
2011, October 2012.

—UEFA Manager of the Year: 1998–99.

—UEFA Team of the Year: 2007, 2008
Onze d'Or Coach of the Year: 1999, 2007, 2008
World Soccer Magazine World Manager of the
Year: 1993, 1999, 2007, 2008.

Sir Alex Ferguson

—European Coach of the Year—Alf Ramsey

Award: 2008.

—IFFHS World's Best Club Coach: 1999, 2008.

—IFFHS World's Best Coach of the 21st

Century: 2012.

—IFFHS All Time World's Best Coach 1996–

2020

—Laureus World Sports Award for Team of the

Year: 2000.

Sir Alex Ferguson

—BBC Sports Personality of the Year Coach
Award: 1999.

—BBC Sports Personality Team of the Year
Award: 1999.

—BBC Sports Personality of the Year Lifetime
Achievement Award: 2001.

—World Soccer Greatest Manager of All Time:
2013.

—ESPN Greatest Manager of All Time: 2013.

—France Football 2nd Greatest Manager of All
Time: 2019.

—Sports Illustrated Greatest Manager of All Time: 2019.

—Globe Soccer Awards Coach of the Century 2001–2020 (2nd among the runners-up).

—BBC Sports Personality Diamond Award: 2013.

—English Football Hall of Fame (Manager): 2002.

—Scottish Football Hall of Fame: 2004.

—European Hall of Fame (Manager): 2008.

—FIFA Presidential Award: 2011.

—Premier League 10 Seasons Awards (1992–93 – 2001–02).

—Manager of the Decade.

—Most Coaching Appearances (392 games).

—Premier League 20 Seasons Awards (1992–93
– 2011–12).

—Best Manager.

—FWA Tribute Award: 1996.

—PFA Merit Award: 2007.

—Premier League Merit Award: 2012–13.

—Mussabini Medal: 1999.

—SFA Special Merit Award: 1985.

—VCGB Scottish Sports Personality of the
Year: 1983.

—Scottish Football Personality of the Year:
1979–80, 1982–83.

Orders and Special Awards

—Officer of the Order of the British Empire (OBE): 1985 New Years Honours List.

—Commander of the Order of the British Empire (CBE): 1995 New Years Honours List.

—Knight Bachelor (Kt.): 1999 Queen's Birthday Honours List.

—Freedom of the City of Aberdeen: 1999.

—Freedom of the City of Glasgow: 1999.

—Freedom of the City of Manchester: 2000.

—Freedom of the Borough of Trafford: 2013.

Honorary Degrees

Ferguson has received at least eight honorary degrees. These Include:

—1996, University of Salford, Master of Arts (MA.)

—December 1997, Robert Gordon University, Doctor of Laws (LL.D).

—2001, Glasgow Caledonian University, Doctorate.

—2002, University of St Andrews, Doctorate.

—2009, Manchester Metropolitan University, Doctor of Business Administration (DBA).

—29 June 2011   University of Stirling

     Doctor of the University (D.Univ).

—12 October 2011, University of Manchester, Doctorate

—2014, Ulster University, Doctor of Science (D.Sc).

Printed in Great Britain
by Amazon

30473700R00086